Wyatt & Sons Publishers books may be ordered through booksellers or by contacting:

Wyatt & Sons Publishers, LLC
Mobile, Alabama 36695
www.wyattpublishing.com
editor@wyattpublishing.com

Because of the dynamic nature of the Internet, any web address or links contained in this book may have changed since publication and may no longer be valid.

Cover design by: Mark Wyatt
Interior design by: Mark Wyatt
ISBN 13:978-1-954798-31-1
Printed in the United States of America

This book was created by the Institute for Disability Studies through its Transition of Teens to Adult Life (ToTAL) program, which is funded through a contract with the Mississippi Department of Rehabilitation Services.

INSTITUTE FOR DISABILITY STUDIES
THE UNIVERSITY OF SOUTHERN MISSISSIPPI

BRIGHT FUTURE!

Written and Illustrated by
Hancock High Self-Advocates

WS
WYATT & SONS
PUBLISHERS, LLC
Mobile, Alabama

Judge Noah

Noah in firetruck

Noah pulled carrots

Noah's first try at photosynthesis

DEDICATION

This book is dedicated to the memory of Noah Charles, whose radiant smile, kind heart, and boundless love brought joy to everyone around him. Writing a book was his dream, and through this publication, that dream has been fulfilled. His light will forever shine in our hearts and in the lives of all those he touched.

Spaceship!
by Kristian Noble

Large, very, very large,
Cyberspace,
Silver and blue
100 mph goes to 160 mph
Maybe we wreck and broken

We ran into alien space rangers and
Were trapped and came up

Crew members
Captain Drake and Communication Officer Hayden
Engineering, Olivia, and the medical staff, Drake
Useful skills we have
Kristian's role is to make food for the crew

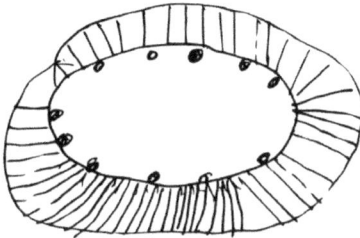

Driver!
by Kristian Noble

Spaceship was a time machine.
To go back and meet Cleopatra and
Rode a horse to Olivia's house

We got back in the spaceship
And came back home.

Spooky House!
by Kristian Noble

Mom, Olivia, Khristopher,
Alexis and Drake
Scooby-doo, Lion Simba and Mufasa
Investigator, a dog and friends
Looking for footprints
Noises night
Scary old ghost
Attic new home

Talking to Animals!
by Kristian Noble

Animals, you can talk to them.
They need help sometimes.
The Veterinarian helps.
Veterinarian helps my cat Riley.
I help my baby dolls. I like to bathe them.

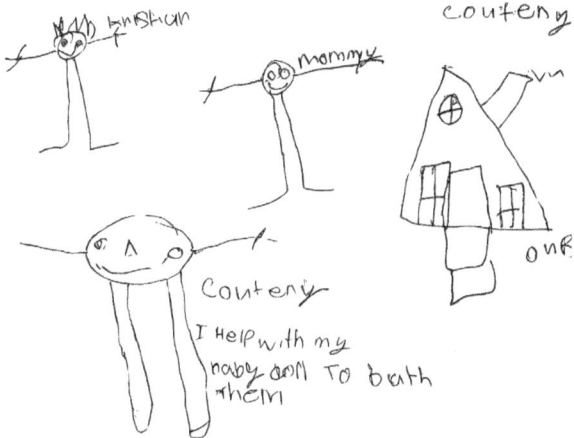

Stranded in space!
by Zachary Geedy

Blue, gas powered,
Holds 8 people
Beds and miles per hour speed
Super-fast, round shape
Kitchen, restroom
Tosha, Drake and Vandercook

Out of gas and the alarm sounds!
Check the ship
Talk to others
Explore and
Build a shelter
Find food maybe?

Talking to Animals!
by Zachary Geedy

Zookeeper
I would say "ZZZZZ"
To the Zebra
It means my name
The Zebra would say
"hey"
I would help the Zebra
By giving him
Some food and a place to live.
The Zebra's name is Zachary, too!

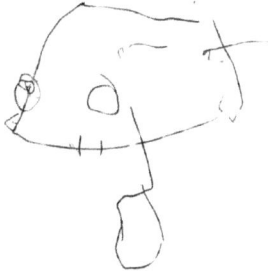

Spooky House!
by Zachary Geedy

Drake and I go to
This haunted house
That had ghostly activity
So, I get the spirit box and
We go check it out

Stranded in Space!
by Collin Clark

7 bedrooms, 1 supply room
2 bathrooms, work drive
Tristan broke the power cell
It is the core of the ship
Captain Collin Clark
Teamwork Mason, Colby and Wyatt

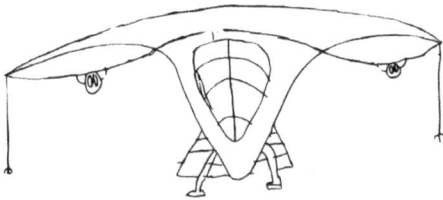

Me and Tony!
by Collin Clark

Collin is the person
Who disarmed traps
Tony is the fighter
Drake is the mapmaker
Time machine watch
Egypt God Osiris

Talking Animals
by Collin Clark

The animals I want to
talk about are Hawks
The Hawks has a hurt wing
So, I call a veterinarian

Factor 57!
by Collin Clark

Earth-like
Mostly birch,
Little wetland
Water stored in
Water bank floor

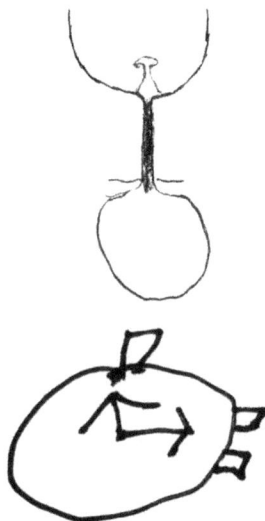

by Collin Clark

Talking Animals
by Perkins Stewart

I will talk to a dog
I will call animal control to assist the dog
The dog said "I need help finding a home"
I tell the dog I will help
The animal control arrives and
I go with them to help
The dog named Clifford
We found Clifford, a new home
He is happy to have a new home

Meghan 2.0
by Perkins Stewart

Alone in the new house 2 found
Meghan 2.0 in the attic
She was left by the previous owner
She comes alive on Alexa
I called the Alexa company for help
They could not help

I called the police too
they came but she was too strong
She gets mad, and I leave
I heard footsteps
I hear her at the door
I locked the door
I get a bucket of water
She breaks in with a fire
I throw the water at her
She is sparking

I bought a new iPhone and
Her spirit went into the phone
My phone started speaking
With her voice
The end

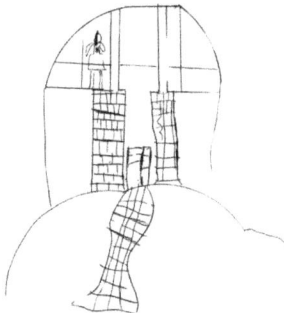

Talking to Animals!
by Caden Voigts

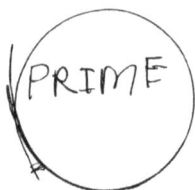

King Von
I want to
Be a
Raptor Prime

Rap Star
by Caden Voigts

Stranded in Space!
by Tristan McCarty

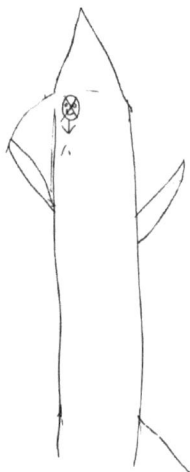

1 million gold
3,000 miles and
Our ship coin hold
Out of gas
Collin Clark, Jakarei,
And Wyatt, Hallie are
Captain problem-solving
Teamwork all
Colby Repair Technician
Use skills needed

Time Machine Egypt Explorer
by Camden Bates

Mom – Treasure hunter
Camden – Time traveler
Dad – Mechanic
Christian – Explorer

We live in Hancock County.

We travel with your time machine to Egypt.
We see pyramids, camels, mummies, elephants.
It was very HOT!

Mom found treasure.

Trapped in Space!
by Colby Walley

The dream supply room, bathroom, wardrobe.
The ship broke. The power cell is the core of the ship.
The Crew
Captain – Collins Clark
Communication Officer – Matt McKane
Medical Staff – Watson
Science Officer – Aila Clark

Talking Animals!
by Mason McFarland

Mason wants
To be
A Zookeeper

Stranded in Space!
by Mason McFarland

Big
Squared
Super-fast
Repair technician
Mason

Spooky House!
by Mason McFarland

My family and I moved to an old mansion on the top of a hill.
I invited Wyatt, Perkins, Harper and Jakarei to camp out
in our attic.
We were telling ghost stories.
We could not sleep.
We turned on all the lights but there were plenty of shadows.

A creaking was coming from the far corner.
And eyes were staring out from the shadows.
Then all the lights went out!
The creaking got louder, and the eyes were coming closer.

We all yelled and hurried down two flights of stairs.
We told my parents, but they just laughed.
Something was fishy!

We stayed awake all night.
Turns out Mom and Dad had hung a fake ghost
On a string with flashing eyes.
It was all fake.

Traveled Back in Time!
by Mason McFarland

A group of my friends and I accidentally
travel back in time to ancient Egypt.
We are trying to find a way back home.

Dustin is stealthy and a science nerd.
Camden, is a master carpenter and artisan,
Jakarei is the navigator and mediator.
He's really cool and dresses snazzy.
Lestat drives the sand boat that
Dustin designed. Plus, he is a history buff
We love adventure!

Camping in Yellow Stone Park!
by Mason McFarland

My friends and I went camping.
After roasting marshmallow plus
Hotdogs we went to sleep.

Lestat began reading about ancient Egypt.
Then he was telling us about it.
He told us about the inside of the pyramids and what
they were for.

Our tent has begun to change.
The next thing I knew we were all inside a pyramid!
The same one Lestat was describing.
I just wanted to go back home.

I began looking for a door.
I could not find one.
It must be 55 B.C.
I looked up to discover the top
the pyramid was not finished.

Camden and Dustin began building a tower so we could
get out.
Jakarei and Lestat talked about how to get back home.
Lestat drew a sand boat while Jakarei made a star map.

Spooky House!
by Jakarei Newkirk

House family
Delilah sees the ghost
Delilah and I ran to
The pumpkin patch and hid.

Planet!
by Jakarei Newkirk

Dear Mars
Too red

Stranded in Space!
by Jakarei Newkirk

Spaceship
Out of gas

Talking Animals!
by Jakarei Newkirk

Save their forest
From destruction
Zookeeper
Kitten Anna

TALKING ANIMALS!
by Wyatt Frye

The animals I would talk to is a Polar Bear
The career that would help me talk to
animals will be a wildlife Biologist
I would talk to a penguin,
wolf, artic fox and a sea cow
I would ask them what their names
And how they survive in the winter climate
And if they lived in other climates
How would they live in those climates

Spooky House!
by Wyatt Frye

I am a monster haunting
Adventure with my friends
Drake, Collin, Hayden
In the spooky house down
the basement the history
Of the house is a mystery
They ran into spirits
In the attic there is
Jason with his hockey mask
Collin ran for his life
Drake was brave
to fight off the monsters
I am going to save them
By just leaving them in the dark
Alone but the werewolf king
Showed up to escape
With my friends

Group of Friends!
by Wyatt Frye

The group of friends' names are
Brayden, Collin, Drake
The job Brayden will have is a map cryptographer.
Collin is the decoder.
Drake is the driver.
Brayden skills are map navigation and directions.
Collin skills are repairing machines and fixing things.
Drake skills are driving trucks, cars and buggies.

Mysterious Portal!
by Wyatt Frye

They found a mysterious portal
The friend's step into the portal and they time travel
back in time to Ancient Egypt in 35 B.C.
They were driving through the desert to find a
secret tomb.

They went inside the tomb and found a time clock
to reverse back to the time they came from.

They were chased by Mummy's on the way back home
to Wyatt's mansion.
And they took the Mummy's to jail!
They saved the day!

The end

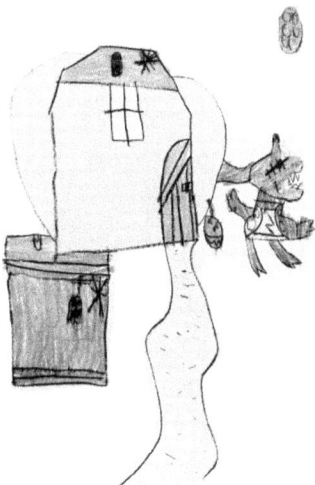

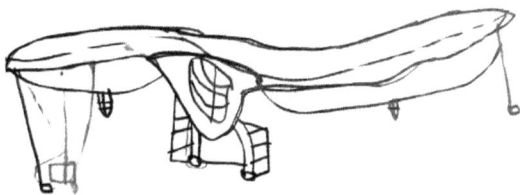

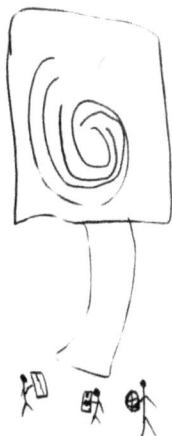

TALKING ANIMALS!
by Lestat Sanders

Lestat is a veterinarian who provides medical care for all kinds of animals.

One day Lestat was hiking ina national forest in Mississippi when suddenly, he was surrounded by a lot of squirrels.

He could understand them! The squirrels were upset because they did not have food for the winter because trees werecut down before their acorns dropped. Help!

Talking Animals
by Hayden Garcia

Tiger
Zookeeper
Feed

Spooky House!
by Hayden Garcia

BIG!
Mom
House
Family
Monster in house werewolf!
The door opened and I got spooked!
The werewolf will scare you.
I used a cane to beat him up.
I called the FBI to get the bad guys.

The Time Machine
by Hayden Garcia

It was a police car.
We traveled to 65 BC, met Cleopatra,
rode a camel and played on a playground.
Then we drove 20 miles and arrived back home.

Stranded in Space!
by Hayden Garcia

Captain Drake 1st command
Hayden 2nd command
It is an extremely large gyrosphere that is red, silver
& blue.
It moves faster than the speed of light & sound.
Aboard there are 20,0000 crew members.
We ran into Alien Space Rangers on one side and
Storm Troopers on the other.
Warp drive is down!

Spooky House!
by Olivia Candebat

My friend Colby is a scientist and Drake is adventurer.
Wyatt explores.
Kristian uncovers.
Perkins was scared!
Hayden spooky.
Alexis's night.
Collin noise.

Lost in Space!
by Olivia Candebat

5,000,000 pounds
21,000 crews
15 rooms and more
Lights flicker, alarms sound
Red lights start blinking!
The spaceship moves faster!
You see other spaceships moving past you.
Other warped drives down!

Talking Animals!
by Olivia Candebat

I like to work as a veterinarian.
Bella Dog and The Fox talk at the Zoo.

The Talking Animals!
by Khristopher Dubose

Olivia Blue Giraffe.

The Talking Animals!
by Drake Ferguson

Owls are special in the United States as Drake is a
Forestry Technician and wants to take care of owls that
need special care every year.
Drake loves eagle owls, barn owls, grey horned owls,
small owls, and snow owls. These owls are special to
him as he takes care of them.
Drake just talks to owls as owls hoot at him, making
them. Drake's owl's name is Hoot Dorno!

Spooky House!
by Drake Ferguson

Drake stays up in an old ancestry house like a wooden cabin as he gets hit by a spirit box and hears the little voice of a 6-year-old child.

Time Machine!
by Drake Ferguson

Braden is a researcher to research old objects or symbols.
Collin is a map reader to find their way to Egypt tombs treasure rooms.
Colby is a booby trap remover to break the traps to make it out alive.
Drake is the leader of the group and a talented driver. They get into the time machine, off road trucker; the lightning strikes and sends them to a big old temple. As the driver hit the brakes to stop, they skid to a stop right on the edge of the cliff! Collin looks at his old map and Braden sets his timer for 2 hours and 25 seconds till a sandstorm strikes.
A final storm starts in the north and south as Colby breaks the traps Drake is getting ready to launch. The full moon reflects the night of trouble, as Collin notices something slithering around in the dark. When suddenly a giant serpent in the shape of a guardian rider appears and Colby is ready to escape as Collin & Braden grab an old spear, they threw them at the serpent. Drake and his group ran back to his time machine as the time is almost out as
The lightning struck the time machine returns them back to their normal time.

31

Lost in Space.
by Drake Ferguson

Extreme long gyrosphere that is red, silver, blue. It moves faster than the speed of light.

A war from space rangers and star troops to anchor 8.

Captain: DTB Commander Hayden (computer Zook) commander

Communication Officer: Khristopher

Navigation: Olivia, Drake

Medical Staff: Olivia

Science Officer: Caden

Kitchen Staff: Kristian

Repair Technician: Drake, Zach, Adorno

Biologists: Caden

Useful Skills Needed

List Skills:

Problem-Solving – Caden, Olivia

Teamwork – Adorno, Drake, Olivia

Communication – Kristian

Adaptability – Drake

Critical Thinking – Kristian

Food prep– Kristian

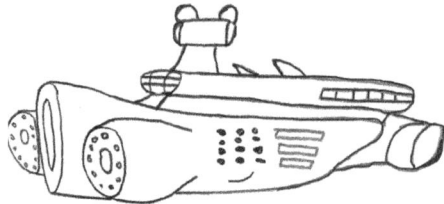

Stranded in Space
by Haley (Hallie) Wallace

You are out of gas!
Goes 3000 miles an hour
1 million miles
The Crew
Captain: Colin
Navigation Officer: Jakarei
Engineering: Wyatt
Medical Staff: Hallie
Kitchen Staff: Collin
Repair Technician: Colby
Biologist: Mason

Problem-Solving – Captain
Communication – All

The Talking Animals!
by Haley (Hallie) Wallace

Deer-Wildlife Conservation Scientist

Warrior Cat!
by Alexis Brown

They are strong, they are mean, they are also mighty
but they can also be kind!

ABOUT THE AUTHORS

Alexis Brown enjoys animals. She likes art and helping others. She wants to own her own pet grooming business.

Caden Voigts likes creating music, especially rap. He hopes to become a rap artist.

Camden Bates is the business owner of Camden Bates Designs. Camden enjoys watching videos, editing, listening to music, creating art, doing puzzles, and hanging out with his family and friends. Camden likes helping others and also plays the piano. He follows a visual or written schedule and likes a well-done to-do list with checkboxes.

Colby Walley enjoys music, gaming, and hanging out with his friends. He would like to become a police officer or work at GameStop.

Collin Clark enjoys playing video games, using virtual reality, and listening to music. He would like to work in a gaming store helping customers to find the items they want.

Drake Ferguson's hobbies include WWE Wrestling, drawing, and telling fascinating stories. He dreams of becoming a WWE Wrestler or a designer.

Haley "Hallie" Wallace enjoys dancing, shopping, hanging out with friends, and watching her favorite TV shows. She is leaning toward a career in the helping professions—possibly as a dance teacher or camp counselor.

Hayden Garcia enjoys playing video games, helping around the house, and cleaning. He is interested in a career in construction.

Jakarei Newkirk likes hanging out with his dad and Delilah. He also enjoys watching videos on his phone and taking pictures and videos. He hopes to have a career in photography or videography.

Khristopher Dubose enjoys spending time with his girlfriend, sister, and friends. He would like to live in Tennessee and have a family. He wants a career in transportation and is working toward getting his driver's license.

Kristian Noble enjoys her dolls, loves to clean, and likes art. She is interested in a career in janitorial services or working in a daycare.

Lestat Sanders enjoys art, food, watching TV, and matching, sorting and categorizing items. He especially loves spending time with his family. Lestat also enjoys opening boxes and sorting objects to be placed on store shelves for purchase. He dreams of working at a bakery where he can help make all things rainbow-colored—especially cakes!

Mason McFarland is 15 years old. He has a dog named Oliver Twist and enjoys using his iPad, watching movies, and going on walks. He is working on communication skills and learning to express himself using his voice.

Noah Charles enjoys watching Mickey's Playhouse, Peppa Pig and Muddy Puddles. His gifts include unique communication skills and impressive handwriting. He is sincerely missed by his fellow students, teachers, and anyone who had the opportunity to know him.

Olivia Candebat likes spending time with her boyfriend and would like to get married someday. She also likes to cook, clean, and draw. Olivia would like a career where she can help others.

Perkins Stewart enjoys learning about cars and trucks. He wants to be a truck driver or a mechanic.

Tristan McCarty enjoys watching TV, playing video games, and sports. He would like a hands-on career such as landscaping, construction, or mechanics.

Wyatt Frye enjoys playing video games, helping others, and drawing. He would like to pursue a career as a video game developer.

Zachary Geedy enjoys playing video games, helping around the house, and cooking. His career goals include becoming a stock clerk in retail or a cook.

You have a story.
We want to publish it.

Everyone has as a story to tell. It might be about something you know how to do, or what has happened in your life, or it may be a thrilling, or romantic, or intriguing, or heartwarming, or suspenseful story, starring a cast of characters that have been swimming around in your imagination.

And at Wyatt & Sons Publishers, we can get your story onto the pages of a book just like the one you are holding in your hand. With professional interior design and a custom, professionally designed cover built just for you from the start, you can finally see your dream of being an author become reality. Then, you will see your book listed with retailers all over the world as people are able to buy your book from wherever they are and have it delivered to their home or their e-reader.

So what are you waiting for? This is your time.

visit us at

www.wyattpublishing.com

for details on how to get started becoming a
published author right away.

www.ingramcontent.com/pod-product-compliance
Lightning Source LLC
Chambersburg PA
CBHW051242020426
42331CB00017B/3488